**At the
Top of
Their
Game**

Ronda
Rousey

Conquering
New Ground

Kevin Snow

**Cavendish
Square**

New York

Published in 2018 by Cavendish Square Publishing, LLC
243 5th Avenue, Suite 136, New York, NY 10016

Copyright © 2018 by Cavendish Square Publishing, LLC

First Edition

Library of Congress Cataloging-in-Publication Data

Names: Snow, Kevin, author.
Title: Ronda Rousey : Conquering New Ground / Kevin Snow.
Description: New York : Cavendish Square Publishing, 2018. | Series: At the Top of Their Game | Includes bibliographical references and index.
Identifiers: LCCN 2016056234 (print) | LCCN 2016059482 (ebook) | ISBN 9781502628329 (library bound) | ISBN 9781502628411 (E-book)
Subjects: LCSH: Rousey, Ronda--Juvenile literature. | Women martial artists--United States--Biography--Juvenile literature.
Classification: LCC GV1113.R69 S66 2018 (print) | LCC GV1113.R69 (ebook) | DDC 796.8092 [B] --dc23
LC record available at "https://lccn.loc.gov/2016056234" https://lccn.loc.gov/2016056234

Editorial Director: David McNamara
Editor: Fletcher Doyle
Copy Editor: Rebecca Rohan
Associate Art Director: Amy Greenan
Designer: Jessica Nevins
Production Coordinator: Karol Szymczuk
Photo Research: J8 Media

Printed in the United States of America

At the Top of Their Game

Contents

Lifelong Fight

It was a brief, nineteen-second sound bite that would leave a lasting impression. In January of 2011, Ultimate Fighting Championship (UFC) Commissioner Dana White was stopped outside of a Los Angeles restaurant by a tabloid news outlet looking for a juicy quote. When the reporter asked if fans would ever see women fighting in UFC, White chuckled as he gave his response.

"Never."

Apparently he'd never met Ronda Rousey. You see, it's always been about the fight for Rousey. But that fight didn't always involve referees, medals, championship belts, or a final decision. For Rousey, the fight has taken on many forms:

The fight to survive right at birth when she was choked by her own umbilical cord.

The fight to overcome her father's suicide when she was just eight years old.

The fight to become the best in the world, spending her teenage years forgoing dances and proms to become one of the top **judoka**

Opposite: Ronda Rousey celebrates her win over Miesha Tate to capture the Strikeforce Women's Bantamweight Championship.

in the United States, ultimately representing her country in two Olympic Games.

The fight to be herself, a war she still wages daily with her own personal demons. Only these days, Rousey's demons are on full display to the world, as she has become one of the most recognizable female athletes on the planet.

Rousey is the fighter that White never expected to encounter. Not only is she a woman, she is talented, beautiful, lethal, focused, and determined. The daughter of a former **judo** world champion, Rousey had been raised and trained in a way that immediately set her apart from those around her.

This is a woman who now knows what she wants out of life; however, it took her a while to figure out what that was. Rousey went through a similar situation in childhood, when her speech was delayed. When she did figure it out, nothing would stand in her way. Words now come as quickly to Rousey as the **knockout** punches she delivers to her opponents.

Rousey has created a global brand for herself based on an idea she had while tending bar. She had recently won a bronze medal at the 2008 Olympic Games in Beijing. Rather than continue along the path that judo had created for her, Rousey craved a new challenge. Not only did she want to pursue a career in **mixed martial arts**, she wanted to be the best in the world. "I can do that," she used to tell herself while watching UFC highlights on television.

Not only did she succeed, but the girl who used to wear a sweatsuit to hide her muscular body is now wearing designer clothes and posing for magazine covers to promote a healthy body image. There was a time when Rousey was living out of her car and didn't even know what she wanted out of life. Now there are little girls who

As a teenager, Ronda Rousey was embarrassed by her muscular body. Now she's proud of who she is and what she has become.

want to grow up to be just like Ronda Rousey. Even after two bad losses, she is still seen as a trailblazer. She may not have realized it when she was going through it, but all the fighting has been worth it.

By the way, don't ever tell Ronda Rousey she can't do something.

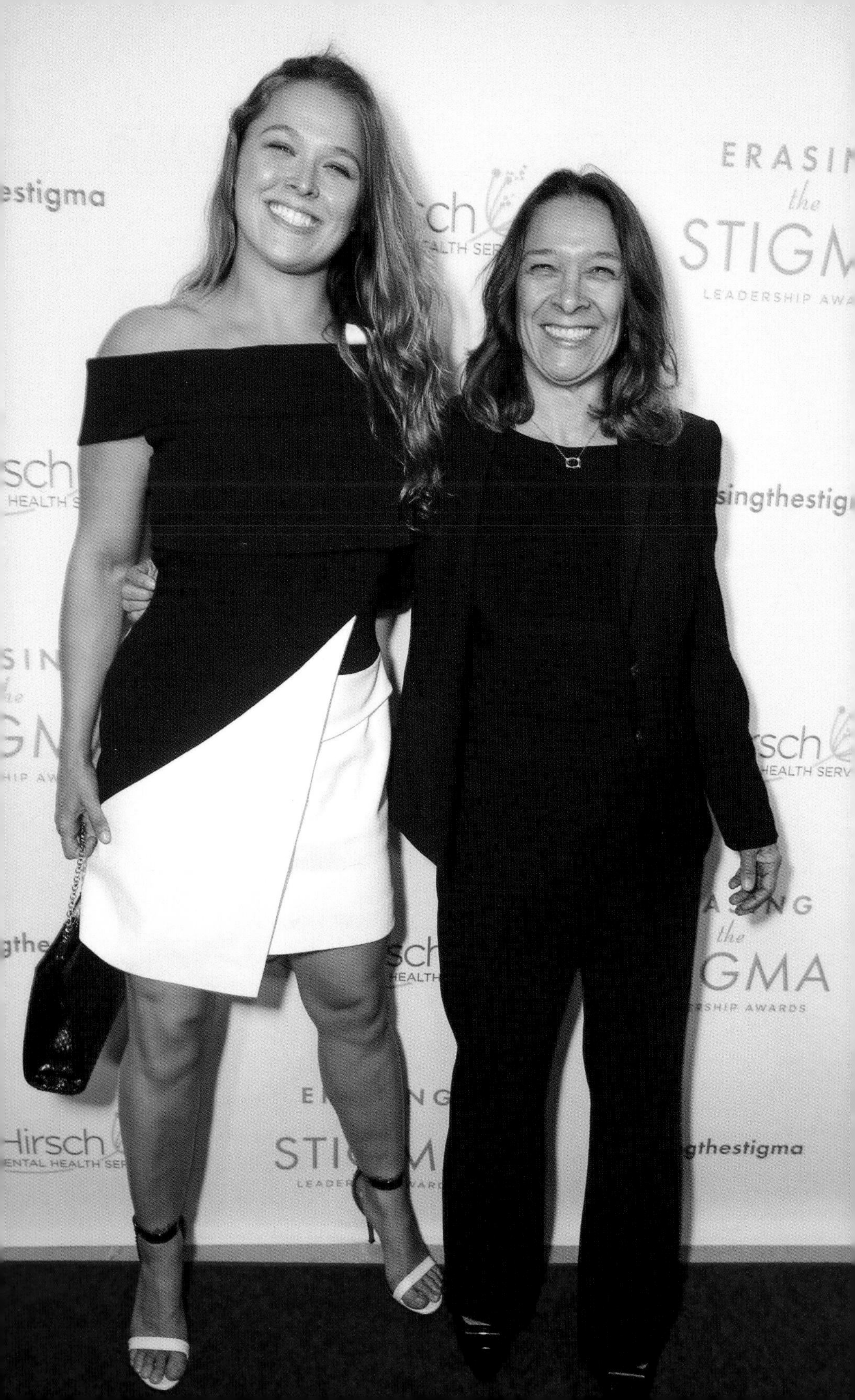
the
Hirsch

Chapter 1

Childhood, and the Fight Begins

Ronda Rousey was born February 1, 1987, in Glenview, California. She was the third daughter of AnnMaria De Mars and Ron Rousey, following Maria and Jennifer.

De Mars was an accomplished athlete. She became the first American to win a gold medal at the Judo World Championships when she prevailed in the 56-kilogram (123-pound) class at the championships in 1984 in Vienna, Austria. At the time she was known as AnnMaria Burns.

After earning her MBA at age twenty-two from the University of Minnesota in 1980, De Mars competed with regular success at major judo events like the **Pan American Championships**, US Senior Nationals, US Collegiate Nationals, and the US Open. De Mars actually came out of retirement in 1984 to win gold at the World championships.

De Mars also earned her PhD in Educational Psychology from the University of California-Riverside. She is currently the CEO of

Opposite: Much of Ronda Rousey's success can be attributed to her training with and the guidance from her mother, AnnMaria De Mars, an accomplished educator, businesswoman, and former judo world champion.

Family is incredibly important to Ronda Rousey, the third of four daughters of AnnMaria De Mars. She's seen here with her younger sister, Julia..

The Julia Group, a small company that provides online education in statistics, mathematics, and disability issues. De Mars is also the founder of 7 Generation Games, a company that creates video games combining math, Native American history, and adventure gaming.

Rousey has described her ethnic background as "half Venezuelan, a quarter English, a quarter Polish, 100 percent American."

Her great-grandfather, Alfred Waddell, was born in Trinidad. He moved in 1928 to Canada, where he would become one of the first black doctors in North America. Waddell had a successful practice in Halifax, Nova Scotia, and his social equality efforts helped provide medical care to many who would have otherwise gone without.

Rousey was named after her father, Ron, an aerospace plant manager. It was Ron who simply left out the "h" in the traditional spelling of the name when providing Ronda's birth name to the nurses at the hospital.

Rousey's arrival into the world wasn't an easy one. Ronda was delivered with her umbilical cord wrapped around her neck. When a baby is born, doctors perform a series of tests to provide what is known as the Apgar Score. A test is completed one minute and five minutes after birth to see how the baby has handled the birthing process. The tested elements include breathing, heart rate, muscle tone, skin color, and reflexes. A normal score ranges from seven to nine out of 10. Rousey was given a score of zero after the initial test.

What followed was a frantic few minutes as doctors struggled to cut the cord and finally provide the blue baby with oxygen. In her 2015 autobiography, Rousey detailed the delivery room panic through her mother's eyes:

Mom says that the doctors thought I was dead. Everything was movement and chaos. Doctors running in from all directions. The squeaking wheels of metal carts carrying equipment being rushed into the room. Cabinets slamming as the medical staff pulled items from the shelves. The lead doctors shouting orders as people poured into the room. Eventually, the doctors managed to get me some air. They cut the cord, unwrapped it from my neck, gave me baby CPR and oxygen. Then after what my mom describes as an eternity—but was probably closer to a few minutes—I started breathing and my heart started beating.

The complications following Rousey's delivery were felt for the first six years of her life as she suffered in silence. The lack of oxygen to her brain during delivery led to a condition called childhood **apraxia** of speech (CAS), a motor speech disorder. Children with CAS have problems saying sounds, syllables, and words. This is not because of muscle weakness or paralysis. The brain has problems planning to move the body parts. The child knows what he or she wants to say, but their brain has difficulty coordinating the muscle movements necessary to say those words. In most cases, the cause is unknown.

Because of the condition, Rousey still wasn't talking by age two and was barely making intelligible sounds at age three. She was constantly undergoing speech therapy, but verbal communication was basically nonexistent for years. It wasn't until she was six years old that Rousey would finally speak in a complete sentence.

Communication Breakdown

The frustration grew inside the house as Rousey would attempt to communicate. Garbled sounds and hand motions became the norm, and as time wore on, her sisters began to pick up on her communication techniques. One incident in particular shows just how frustrating it had become.

Watching World Wrestling Federation (WWF) events on television had become a Saturday morning staple for Rousey and her sisters. The three of them (Julia was not yet born) would watch each week, then reenact their favorite moves on the couch and carpet.

When Rousey turned three, her parents asked her what she wanted for her birthday. Being such a wrestling fan, she had her eyes on a Wrestling Buddy, a 2-foot (61 centimeter) tall pillow designed in the shape of your favorite WWF superstar. Rather than tossing her sisters around, Rousey wanted to wrestle with her own stuffed buddy. Since her favorite wrestler was Hulk Hogan, the decision was easy as to which one she wanted.

"Balgrin," she repeated over and over to her parents when they asked what she wanted. Not knowing who or what "Balgrin" was, the entire family loaded into the car and set out in search of the mysterious birthday gift. They visited every toy store in Riverside and Los Angeles Counties searching for "Balgrin," scouring the aisles as if they were on a treasure hunt. Yet they continued to come up empty.

Their last stop of the day was at a Toys "R" Us store. Rousey's father spoke to one of the store clerks and explained that his daughter wanted a "Balgrin" for her birthday. The clerk asked a few questions, wondering if he knew any more specific details about the toy. Since Rousey was the only one who knew what "Balgrin" was, she began explaining in the only way she knew how, repeatedly throwing herself to the ground like a wrestler would. After giving it some more thought, the clerk finally figured out the mystery. Rousey described the exchange in her autobiography.

"Do you mean a Wrestling Buddy? It's like a pillow and you wrestle with it."

I nodded slowly. "Balgrin," I said.

"Right," he replied as if I'd spoken clear as day, "Hulk Hogan."

The family moved from Southern California to Minot, North Dakota, when Rousey was three years old. De Mars had received a job offer from Minot State University, the third-largest university in the state. An immediate benefit of the move would be Rousey's opportunity to take advantage of the school's renowned speech pathology program.

The family had gone from the hustle and bustle of life in California, to a sprawling farm home on 5 acres (2 hectares) of land twenty minutes outside of Minot. The newfound freedom turned out to be heaven for Rousey and her sisters. They would spend hours roaming the property, exploring nature and simply being kids. Rousey really took to country life and developed a passion for rock collecting. Her father would help her identify the samples she would bring home each day.

Rousey and her father would develop a close bond during their time in North Dakota. With De Mars off at school and her sisters occupied with other things, "Ronnie" and Ron would spend hours each day together on rock-hunting adventures or just exploring the area in their Ford Bronco.

Winter of Pain

The first winter in North Dakota meant the first experience with frigid temperatures and snow for the entire family. That wasn't the only change. Ron Rousey had retired when the family left California, then decided he wanted to return to work. A few months after their arrival in North Dakota, Rousey's parents were forced to live separately when her father took a job at a manufacturing plant in Devils Lake. It was about 120 miles (193 km) from Minot. He returned home each weekend to be with his wife and kids.

On one of his weekend visits during a cold January spell, the Rouseys went sledding. As the family watched from the top of the hill along with their friends, Rousey's father was the first one to make a trip down, explaining that he would check out the run to see if it was safe for the others.

The seemingly uneventful run ended with a bump over a snow-covered log at the bottom of the hill. The sled came to a complete stop, and Rousey's father also wasn't moving. Thinking he was joking around, the group went down the hill to check on him. A call for help was made, with two ambulances arriving soon after. It was quickly determined that he'd suffered a broken back.

Ron Rousey would remain in the hospital for five months, his recovery complicated by a rare bleeding disorder (Bernard-Soulier syndrome) that resulted in excessive postoperative bleeding from the trauma suffered and the numerous surgeries that followed. He was taken to a hospital in Bismarck because the hospital in Minot couldn't handle an injury of this severity. De Mars would take Rousey and her sisters to visit their father every day after school, making the 130-mile (209 km) drive each way five times a week.

He wouldn't be released from the hospital until the spring of 1991, and now he had a metal rod in his spine. In 1993, the family moved again when AnnMaria De Mars took a job at the University of Jamestown.

With Rousey's speech issues not improving, her speech therapist recommended that she live with her father in Devils Lake. Through no fault of her own, Rousey had become somewhat dependent on her sisters to help her communicate. When she struggled to express herself, one of the sisters would often step in and speak up on her behalf. They became familiar with Rousey's verbal and nonverbal cues and would translate so she could communicate with others.

In the eyes of the therapist, that had to change. The one-on-one time with her father would help develop her speech, as she'd be forced to communicate on her own. It was during this time that Rousey truly became daddy's girl. They'd already started getting close before the accident, but now it was just the two of them. They'd watch movies together, talk about everything, and at the end of each day, they'd sit together and watch the animal documentary series, *Wild Discovery*. Rousey still credits her love and knowledge of animals to the hours spent watching this show with her father.

Ron Rousey encouraged his daughter to take part in a local swimming club, where she developed a passion for the sport. He also spoke to Rousey in a way that comforted her about her speech problems.

He said to her: "Don't you worry about it. You are going to show everyone one day. You're just a sleeper. You know what a sleeper is? A sleeper just waits and when the time is right, they come out and wow everyone. That's you, kiddo. Don't you worry."

Pain and Suffering

By the time Ronda turned eight years old, her speech had become increasingly clear but her father's pain only got worse. His damaged spine wasn't getting better and there was nothing any doctor could do about it. He'd hid the pain from the family for a while, and doctors told him he would be paralyzed within a matter of years.

With the pain forcing Ron to quit his job, the family moved back in together in Jamestown. The girls thought nothing of their father's pain as he just went about his business of being their dad. Ronda was just happy to have her dad around during her summer vacation. But as he masked the pain in his back from the girls, nothing could hide the growing pain in his heart. Her father was a proud man who couldn't bear the thought of being unable to help raise his daughters and support the family.

On the afternoon of August 11, 1995, after calling his wife one final time, Ron Rousey drove to the pond where he and his youngest daughter often spent time together. After attaching a tube to the tailpipe, he brought the open end into the car and rolled up the window. The pain had become too much to handle. He committed suicide by **asphyxia**.

Ronda Rousey was just young enough to be somewhat oblivious to the events that followed—the crush of family and friends, the visitation, the funeral, and all the emotions. She still describes it as like being in a haze for a while. She wrote in her autobiography:

> I did the best I could just to keep going. Sometimes it
> felt like Dad wasn't home from work yet. ... But after

a while him not being there started to seem normal. I still missed my dad. I still thought about him every day—I still think about him every day—but I knew not to expect him to walk through the door.

Chain of Events

Rousey remained in North Dakota with her mother and sisters until 1998, when they moved back to California. De Mars had remarried in 1997, and would have a fourth daughter, Julia, with her new husband in March of 1998. The family settled in Santa Monica, where De Mars worked multiple jobs to help support her kids and their numerous activities.

After the turmoil of the final years in North Dakota, life in California was becoming normal for Rousey and her sisters. Just like any siblings, they were always at war about something. Quite often those battles would turn physical, as they did in the early days in the living room watching WWF on television and launching themselves off the furniture.

De Mars even recalls one fight where an entire set of encyclopedias was involved, along with an office chair that was ready to be launched from the top of the stairs.

"They would fight over everything; who got the prize in the cereal box, and then Ronda would cry, because she cries over everything," said De Mars. "That doesn't bother me because I'm so used to it, but she would be crying and punching them, and then they'd be in this fistfight in the living room."

Considering some of the epic victories their younger sister has claimed in recent years, it's very possible that Maria and Jennifer may

Family Pride

To this day, her father's suicide is not something that Ronda Rousey likes to discuss in interviews. That's why it became so newsworthy prior to her fight at UFC 190 in Brazil, in August 2015, when her opponent, Bethe Correia, made a suicide reference in her pre-fight comments.

"She is not mentally healthy, she needs to take care of herself," Correia said. "She is winning, so everybody is around her cheering her up, but when she realizes she is not everything that she believes she is, I don't know what might happen. I hope she does not kill herself later on."

An enraged Rousey fired back immediately at Correia, who later tried to deny any knowledge of Rousey's father's suicide.

"She already got the fight," Rousey said. "There was already enough heat behind the fight. It was entirely unnecessary. To bring my family into it, they don't

An elated Ronda Rousey defeated previously unbeaten Bethe Correia at UFC 190 in Brazil.

deserve that and they didn't ask for that. I need to make sure nobody else tries that ever again."

Rousey pummeled Correia via TKO just thirty-four seconds into the first round of her fourth title defense.

have had more success than most women when it comes to battling Ronda Rousey.

De Mars wasn't always around to supervise her daughters. Not long after marrying her second husband, Dennis, she had to leave town for a few days on a business trip. She wanted the oldest daughter, Maria, to ease Dennis into the situation considering he'd never been married or had kids before. Her basic instructions were to keep the warring sisters at bay. Easier said than done.

"So, I call up and say, 'How are things?' Dennis was just at a loss for words. He says, 'Well, they all got into a fistfight at the kitchen table.'"

Maria and Ronda got into it about something, and Ronda spit in her face. That prompted Maria to slap Ronda, and then Jennifer even got involved for reasons that De Mars still can't understand. From there, it turned into a full-blown brawl.

De Mars then yelled at each of her daughters over the phone. She was most upset with Maria, because she had specifically asked her to play peacemaker that night. When it came time to punish Ronda, De Mars was at a loss for words. Ronda immediately started pleading her case with her mother, because in her mind, she'd done nothing wrong.

"I grounded Ronda too, and then she starts arguing with me, saying 'I shouldn't be grounded because you didn't specifically tell me not to spit in Maria's face.'"

One of the rules De Mars had in her house was that you could only hit someone if they hit you first. That rule also carried over to the schoolyard, where Rousey often found herself to be the target of bullies. Ronda was a skinny kid and appeared to be an easy mark, for both boys and girls. But regardless of how much she was taunted, Rousey could never throw the first punch.

One afternoon in sixth grade, a boy approached her from behind and grabbed her throat. His grip got so tight that it was becoming difficult for Rousey to breathe. However, the boy had no idea that his victim had been taking judo lessons. He found out quickly when he was hip tossed and his head slammed down on the concrete. Embarrassed by what had just happened, the bleeding boy quickly left the scene. It wasn't until later that he ended up going to a medical professional for stitches.

When De Mars came to pick up her daughter from school that day, the dumbfounded principal let Rousey go home without any form of punishment.

Chapter 2

Beginning of the Rise

With a mother considered to be one of the most talented female judoka of her generation, it only seems fitting that Rousey turned to the sport during one of the darkest times of her childhood. Judoka is the term used to describe someone that takes part in judo.

Having captured United States and Pan American judo titles, De Mars gained international recognition in 1984 by becoming the first American—man or woman—to win gold at the World Judo Championship in Vienna, Austria. De Mars's relentless and attacking style was admired by teammates and feared by her opponents. She specialized in **submissions** and possessed a devastating ground attack. De Mars documented these techniques in her 2013 book, *Winning on the Ground: Training and Techniques for Judo and MMA Fighters*, considered by many as one of the top judo teaching tools.

Rousey was almost eleven years old when her mother first convinced her to try judo. It had been three years since her father's death, and the bitterness still lingered. Rousey had become a

Opposite: California's Glendale Fighting Club became a second home for Ronda Rousey while she honed her combat skills.

talented swimmer, taking part in competitions throughout North Dakota. Her father had been her biggest fan, and the thought of continuing to swim sickened her. Rousey needed an outlet, and as she did with all of her children, De Mars introduced her to judo in 1998.

Rousey was hooked instantly. She wrote:

> The very first time I stepped on the judo mat I fell in love with the sport. I was amazed at how complex judo was. How creative you had to be. There are so many little parts and so much thought that goes into every move and technique. I love the problem-solving aspect of fighting. It's about feeling and understanding and breaking down an opponent. It's not just 'go faster.'

Despite being scrawny as a kid, Rousey displayed her judo talents early on. Her natural abilities took over and developed quickly under her mother's teachings. De Mars's characteristic ground attack and lethal submission holds immediately became a staple of Rousey's repertoire.

"My style came from my mom and my early coaching," she told Bleacher Report. "My mom tore her knee out when she was seventeen, and they didn't have any ACL [anterior cruciate ligament] reconstruction or anything back then. She wanted to stay with judo, so she had to have an exclusive ground game. My mom was really innovative in the judo world. She was the first woman to really spend any time on strength and conditioning. And the first to spend a lot of time on the ground."

Just weeks after taking up the sport, Rousey won her first tournament, which took place on her eleventh birthday. Rousey was a runner-up in her second tournament, then experienced some tough love from her mother.

At the conclusion of her final match, the opposing coach approached Rousey and offered congratulations on her performance in a losing effort. Rousey appreciated the kind words until catching her mother's eye immediately afterward. De Mars took Rousey aside and told her the coach's words were hollow, and she shouldn't feel content with a second-place finish. The one-way conversation went on for several minutes, with De Mars repeatedly telling Rousey she should be upset with losing, not just accepting of her effort.

Her mother's words hit Rousey hard, and left an immediate impact. She later said:

> I was ashamed that I had been so ready to accept losing, to accept as fact that someone else was simply better than me. The remorse lasted only a second before it was replaced by a more intense emotion. What I felt then was a deep desire to win, a motivation to show everyone on the planet that no one should ever doubt my ability to win again. From that moment on, I wanted to win every time I stepped onto the mat. I expected to win. I would never accept losing again.

The only thing that seemed to be able to slow Rousey in the early stages of her career was an injury.

Rousey skipped classes one day during her sophomore year of high school in 2003 and broke her left foot when landing on it the wrong way while jumping a fence. She was scheduled to compete in a local club tournament the next day and went ahead with her matches despite the throbbing pain in her swollen foot.

Rousey would win the double-elimination tournament, but was subsequently grounded for a month by her mother when she revealed the reasons behind her injury.

That was followed in April by a torn ACL suffered while sparring at her gym. While still favoring the previously broken left foot, Rousey got hit by her training partner on the right knee and dropped immediately. It took a full day of prodding by Rousey's coaches to convince her mother to get the knee looked at by a doctor, where the ACL tear was diagnosed. Rousey had the tear surgically repaired a few days later and was instructed to stay off her leg for a period of months before returning to training. That didn't stop her mother from getting her back into action just one week later, reminding her that she could still work on other things while rehabbing her right knee. While she wouldn't compete for six months, Rousey used this time to improve her ground game and overall matwork.

Improving Her Techniques

De Mars knew that if her daughter was going to continue developing her techniques, it would mean having to send her to another coach. There's only so much you can learn from one coach, especially when the coach's voice you're hearing all the time is also your mother's.

Even though De Mars had her doubts, the next stop for Rousey would be the famed Hayastan Academy in North Hollywood. The Hayastan Academy is an international destination for martial arts training, specializing in judo, sambo, wrestling, grappling, boxing, kickboxing, and mixed martial arts (MMA). Hayastan has become a world-renowned training center for judo and grappling and has produced many of the top MMA fighters in the UFC and other professional organizations.

Gokor Chivichyan runs the Academy, and his resume is full of international success stories. The Armenian-born Chivichyan came to Los Angeles at age seventeen after an impressive run of titles in judo, sambo and wrestling. His first trainer in the United States was the legendary Gene LeBell. LeBell was a martial arts instructor who became known for his work in professional wrestling. He also worked as a stuntman in more than 240 movies and many television shows, performing with everyone from Bruce Lee and Chuck Norris to Elvis Presley and Steven Seagal.

When the Academy opened in 1991, Chivichyan retired from competition to run the club along with LeBell. It was at the Academy where Rousey met Manny Gamburyan. The two became training partners, and Gamburyan would regularly push Rousey to her limits physically and mentally. Gamburyan would go on to a successful career in UFC and continues to train with Rousey.

Rousey was able to train on a limited basis at Hayastan throughout her recovery from her knee injury but was forced to miss both the 2003 Senior Nationals and the Junior US Open. Doubt crept into her mind, and Rousey wondered if her future dream was disappearing before her eyes.

She undertook a rigorous training regimen and returned to make her senior international debut at the US Open in Las Vegas, losing the title match on points to Great Britain's Sarah Clark. One week later she won the Rendez-vous Canada event in Montreal, defeating thirty-year-old Australian veteran Carly Dixon in the finals. Six months after having her ACL repaired, Rousey's run of success made her the top-ranked woman in the United States in the women's 63-kg (139 pound) division at age sixteen.

Legendary trainer Gene LeBell has been a mentor to Ronda Rousey throughout her career, and worked with her at the Hayastan MMA Academy in North Hollywood, California.

Number One with a Bullet

Competing in the 2008 **Summer Olympics** had always been Rousey's goal. However, her rapid rise to the top suddenly brought the 2004 Games into view. Shortly after turning seventeen, Rousey won the 2004 Pan American Championships and the US National Championships. In some matches she was dispatching competitors twice her age.

One of Rousey's main rivals in the spring of 2004 was thirty-nine-year-old Grace Jividen, who had actually been a teammate of De Mars back in 1981. Jividen had held the top spot in the 63-kilogram (139 pound) division until being unseated by the teenaged Rousey at the US National Championships in San Diego.

The two would square off again six weeks later at the **Olympic Trials** in Colorado Springs. Rousey defeated Jividen by **ippon** in the finals, ensuring her spot on the Olympic team and a trip to Athens. In judo, an ippon is a winning point that is awarded for using a perfectly executed technique. Not only was the seventeen-year-old Rousey the youngest member of the US judo team in Athens, she was the youngest judo competitor in the Games.

Despite having origins that date back to the 1800s, women's judo didn't make its first appearance at the Olympics until the 1988 Summer Games in Seoul, South Korea. Even then it was a demonstration event, with no medals awarded. Judo didn't become an official medal event until the Barcelona Games in 1992. On an international level, women's judo didn't even have a World Championship until 1980 at Madison Square Garden in New York City.

Heading East

Wakefield is a small town a little more than 12 miles (19 km) north of downtown Boston, Massachusetts. It is the home of Pedro's Judo Center, run by **sensei** "Big Jim" Pedro and his son, Jimmy Jr. At her mother's behest, a teenaged Ronda Rousey moved to Wakefield in January 2004 to live and train with the Pedros to prepare for her Olympic judo quest. She had met the Pedros during her rehab.

Big Jim was a five-time World team coach and a bronze medalist at the 1974 Pan American Championships. Jimmy Jr. won Olympic bronze medals for Team USA in 1996 and 2004 and took home bronze at the 1991 and 1995 World Championships.

"She was a cagey fighter," Jimmy Jr. said of Rousey in a 2015 interview with SkySports.com. "There are only a few people who truly hate losing more than they enjoy winning."

Rousey spent the first few weeks living with Jimmy Jr. and his wife before moving to Big Jim's small house in rural New Hampshire. It was a solitary but focused existence for Rousey. She spent several hours each day grinding through rigorous practices and training sessions. Rousey struggled with the quiet lifestyle but realized that she'd never been in a better place with judo, both physically and mentally.

Jimmy Jr. says he still sees that focus in Rousey today.

"What's happening today is that you have Ronda, who is a devastatingly trained assassin, fighting against girls who have only recently started trying to catch up to something that she's practiced for her whole life. Their instincts just aren't there."

Rena Kanokogi, who won a YMCA judo tournament in 1959 disguised as a man, mortgaged her home to help pay for that first women's World Championship tournament. Kanokogi was one of the driving forces to get women's judo introduced at the 1988 Olympics, and she coached the US Women's Team that year.

The Olympic Experience

Rousey tried to soak in as much as she could during her first Olympic experience, but the competitor in her spent most of the time focusing on the task at hand. Rousey would lose her first match to Claudia Heill of Austria, the eventual silver medalist. Moving into the **repechage** bracket, her next opponent was Clark, in a rematch from the US Open championship final.

Being in the repechage bracket meant the best Rousey could do now was a bronze medal, but she'd have to win the rest of her matches. Rousey avenged the US Open loss with a victory over Clark and moved on to face Hong Ok-song of Korea. This is where Rousey's Olympic journey would end, losing on points to the Korean. Rousey finished ninth overall in Athens, the best placing of any woman on the US team.

For someone as intense as Rousey, her Olympic finish was devastating. She wasn't trained to finish ninth overall and be satisfied with the result, even though it was her first Olympics and she was only seventeen. Rousey didn't even stick around Athens for the Closing Ceremonies, flying home as quickly as she could once her competition was done.

The first major event in which Rousey competed following the Olympics was the 2004 World Junior Championships in Budapest. Because of her age, Rousey was able to compete in both junior- and

Ronda Rousey battles Austria's Claudia Heill, the eventual silver medalist, at the 2004 Olympics at seventeen years of age.

Ronda Rousey: Conquering New Ground

senior-level tournaments. With the anger of the Olympics still at the forefront of her mind, Rousey was determined to show the under-20 world what she was really all about.

She ran roughshod over her competition, winning all three of her matches on the first day to advance to the semifinals. She faced nineteen-year-old Irina Gromova of Russia in the semifinals and handily dispatched her on points. Up next for the championship was China's Jing Jing Mao, who had also gone undefeated in her four matches. Rousey won the gold medal in dominating fashion, slamming Mao for the victory just four seconds into the match.

Personal Pressures

Rousey's winning ways continued throughout 2005. She won five of the seven tournaments she entered, including both the Pan American and US National Championships. However, while she was succeeding on the mat, her personal life was in turmoil.

Her coaches questioned her focus, while her mother had taken issue with how seriously Rousey was pursuing her GED online. De Mars became so outraged with Rousey's attitude that she wanted her daughter to take a year off from judo, finish high school, and experience life in the real world. One coach had already sent her home, and then Rousey packed up in the middle of the night and left her mother's house. She lived with friends in Upstate New York for a while, along with stops in Montreal and Chicago. The pressures that came with Rousey's athletic success were suddenly clashing with the ideals of a teenager who simply felt lost in all the chaos. But as emotions swirled on both sides, Rousey was able to regain her focus and passion for training.

Looking back on it now, Rousey knows she probably could've handled the situations better. "I think I definitely went the wrong way. I really hurt a lot of people," she said.

In April of 2006, Rousey became the first American woman in nine years to win a World Cup tournament, as she was victorious in all five of her matches at the World Cup in Birmingham, England. A few weeks later she took home gold at the US Senior Nationals in Houston. After winning the Pan American Championship title in 2005, Rousey followed that up with a second-place finish at the 2006 event in Argentina.

A string of three straight tournament wins in the fall made Rousey the prohibitive favorite at the 2006 World Junior Championships in Santo Domingo, Dominican Republic. After a frustrating opening-match loss, Rousey was forced to battle her way through the repechage bracket to win a bronze medal. This made her the first US athlete to win two medals at the Junior Worlds.

A Weighty Issue

Making weight had always been a struggle for Rousey, but the problem was increasing by 2006. Rousey was five feet three inches tall (1.6 m) when she started competing at the 63-kg (138 pound) weight class in 2003 as a sixteen-year-old. Four years had passed and she now stood at five feet seven inches (1.7 m), and normally checked in around 160 pounds (72 kg) when she wasn't competing. This meant she'd have to drop 22 pounds (9 kg) prior to every tournament. Rousey now couldn't handle the physical and mental toll it was taking on her to make weight.

After vomiting during a match at the British Open in January 2007 (a tournament she'd eventually win), Rousey decided she'd had enough. When she competed at the World Cup in Austria three weeks later, Rousey entered at the 70-kg (154 pound) class. Not only did she win the tournament, she had fun doing it.

"I realized that the making weight part of competition had become the whole tournament for me. Once that wasn't an issue anymore, my focus was just on competing and having fun."

Rousey's sights were now firmly set on the 2008 Olympics. Her gold medal win at the 2007 Pan American Championships was highlighted by a semifinal victory over the 6-foot (1.9 meters) Edith Bosch from the Netherlands, the reigning 70-kg world champion.

In the ten events Rousey entered in 2007, she had top three finishes in all of them, including six gold medals. Rousey also became the first American woman in twelve years to earn a World Championship medal by finishing second. Everything was setting up nicely for what would unfold at the Olympics in Beijing.

Redemption Time

Rousey won three of her five tournaments in 2008 prior to the Olympics, including the US Nationals and US Olympic Trials. Following the trials, Rousey had two full months to prepare for her moment of redemption.

August 13 would be Rousey's day of reckoning, as the entire competition would be decided in one day at the Beijing Science and Technology University Gymnasium. Rousey opened the tournament with convincing wins over Nasiba Surkieva (Turkmenistan) and Katarzyna Pilocik (Poland). That set up her up for a quarterfinal match with Bosch. The two women fought hard, battling to a scoreless regulation after five minutes. Next was the "golden score" five-minute overtime where any point would decide

The 2008 Olympics brought a much different result for Rousey, as she fought her way through the repechage bracket to win a bronze medal.

the match. With the overtime nearing an end, Bosch turned Rousey on her back for the match-winning point.

Just like in 2004, Rousey would now be forced to fight her way through the repechage bracket, needing three wins for a bronze medal. After wins over opponents from Algeria and Hungary, Rousey faced Germany's Annett Böhm with a bronze medal at stake. Böhm had won a bronze at the 2004 Games.

Rousey needed the full five minutes to defeat Böhm on points, becoming the first American to win an Olympic medal in women's judo since it became an Olympic sport in 1992. The pain of her 2004 Olympic failure was finally erased in a way that Rousey never would have expected.

"I had not won a gold medal but there was a sense of accomplishment I never would have believed could come from third place," she said. "Of all the third-place finishes in my career, the bronze in the Olympics was the only one I took any satisfaction in."

Chapter 3

A Land of Confusion

Rousey returned home to California from the 2008 Summer Olympics with the weight of the world literally off her shoulders. Ten years after she first stepped onto a judo mat, Rousey was finally free. All the hours of training had finally resulted in the Olympic medal that she wanted so badly. And now the Olympic medalist was coming home.

But to what? The man she had dated before the Olympics had moved on to someone else in her absence, so she had no place to live and no job.

Rousey's triumphant return from Olympic glory wasn't what she had expected. Rousey had already made up her mind that she wanted to take a break from judo after Beijing and spend a year enjoying herself as just a regular person. What she didn't realize was how much her life had been dictated by her constant training and competition schedule. The years of training had come to a screeching halt. She no longer had to care what she put into her

Opposite: Ronda Rousey took home a bronze medal in the 2008 Olympics, becoming the first US woman to win a medal in judo since its inception into the Olympics in 1992.

body—both good and bad. The structure that she had become so accustomed to disappeared in the blink of an eye.

Even before leaving Beijing, Rousey posted this comment on her blog: "I dunno, maybe I'm stressing about nothing. I'm at the Olympic village, have finished fighting, have no responsibilities, waking up at 2 p.m. and not the slightest clue of what day or date it is."

Rousey's post-Olympics emotions are nothing new for athletes competing in the world's largest sporting event. Regardless of the sport, athletes endure years of meticulous training to prepare for their moment in the intense glare of the spotlight.

Just like Rousey was in Athens, gymnast Shawn Johnson was a teenager when she competed at the 2008 Summer Olympics. The sixteen-year-old Johnson became America's darling in Beijing by winning a gold medal on the balance beam and capturing three silver medals in the floor exercise, team, and all-around competitions.

"I remember waking up the next day after my last competition and feeling like I had run straight into a brick wall," Johnson explained in a story that appeared in the *Washington Post* on August 20, 2016. "As an elite athlete you obsess; you're a perfectionist over your field. And when you don't have that to devote every ounce of energy to every day, it's hard. Any elite athlete will tell you: the transition from Olympics into normal life is so hard."

Steven Ungerleider is a sports psychologist and author who has done extensive work with the International Olympic Committee (IOC) and the US Olympic Committee (USOC) for more than forty years. Whether it's days, weeks, or years later, transitioning to the real world is an incredibly difficult thing to do for many Olympic athletes.

Like many Olympic athletes, gymnast Shawn Johnson struggled to adjust to everyday life after winning four medals at the 2008 Summer Olympics in Athens.

"It's an emotional, psychological transition, and it's very tough," Ungerleider said in that *Washington Post* story. "We're always seeing a large number of athletes who win medals, or don't win medals, and come home, the lights are turned out, the media is gone, and they go into a state of shock because they have been up on the pedestal and this emotional high for so long. And without their training regimen and support staff, it's a tough transition."

Rousey's reward from the USOC for winning bronze was $10,000. The after-tax haul was $6,000, and she used of all of that to buy a used Honda Accord—and still had to finance the remainder. That car would also serve as her apartment on a few occasions early on when money was tight.

Rousey had come to despise the regimented training lifestyle that had ruled her existence for the last decade. For the better part of the next year, she wanted no part of any schedules or rules. There would be no weigh-ins or random IOC drug tests. She could stay out as late as she wanted, doing whatever she wanted, with whomever she wanted. This was her "normal" life to live and she wanted to live it on her terms.

Returning to Normal

There was no glory attached to Rousey's new lifestyle. Even with two Olympic appearances to her credit, Rousey was just another bartender at one of the three restaurants on her work schedule. When she finally found time to sleep, her home was a tiny studio apartment with constant plumbing problems.

The Olympic dream that had captivated Rousey since she was a child had turned her life into a meaningless nightmare. Despite winning a bronze medal, the end didn't justify the means in Rousey's mind.

"I had endured so much to get to the Olympics. All along the way, I told myself the result would be amazing: that it would all be worthwhile. But the truth was it had been amazing, but it hadn't been worth it. Realizing that crushed me. I had dreamed of the Olympics since I was a little girl. I won an Olympic medal, and yet I felt like I had been let down."

It took a year, but eventually the competitor in her returned. There was a time when she contemplated training for the 2012 Olympics, but she hated the idea of sinking back into that lifestyle for another three years. Her mother was pushing Rousey towards college and possibly even resurrecting her aquatic background to become a helicopter rescue swimmer for the Coast Guard.

However, there was one idea that started percolating in the back of her mind: becoming a mixed martial arts fighter. While tending bar at night, Rousey would find herself watching MMA highlights on TV. Each time she would get the same thought in her mind: I can do that.

At the urging of Manny Gamburyan, one of her former training partners, Rousey returned to the gym. Gamburyan had kept in touch with Rousey since she got back from the Olympics, but the timing just seemed right. "Judo hadn't made me happy," she said. "But not doing judo wasn't making me happy either. I worried nothing would ever make me happy, that I'd missed my chance at happiness."

Upon returning to the gym, Rousey realized that the lure was about more than just judo. The rise in popularity of MMA had taken hold of many fighters at the gym, including Gamburyan. He was a former judo competitor who had just signed a contract with UFC.

Retired UFC fighter Manny Gamburyan (*center*) has worked closely with Rousey from her early days at the Hayastan Academy.

Ronda Rousey: Conquering New Ground

Rousey had briefly considered a judo comeback. She had even concocted a training plan that would allow her to do both judo and MMA, looking toward her future after the 2012 Olympics. In Rousey's mind, judo would benefit in the long run if she were to become an MMA champion. She even approached Jimmy Pedro Jr. about becoming her coach in this plan. Pedro declined the offer.

However, after competing in a few international judo events, she started having the same empty feelings about the sport that had consumed her in the past. Despite her talent, she wasn't prepared to spend the next three years doing something that had already made her miserable. The lure of making actual money in MMA was also very appealing to Rousey, rather than the minimal stipend that had been provided to her by the US Judo Federation in recent years.

There was just something intoxicating to Rousey about MMA. She already possessed the natural quickness and agility from judo. Now she was able to incorporate elements of boxing, along with the knee and elbow strikes from **muay thai**, the national sport and cultural martial art of Thailand. Muay thai is a discipline that uses stand-up striking in combination with various clinching techniques. It is a form of close combat that was developed several hundreds of years ago that utilizes the entire body as a weapon.

Putting the Wheels in Motion

As Rousey began to focus her attention full-time on an MMA career, she decided the next step was getting a manager to help her book fights. She would continue training, while the manager would take the reins of promoting her and finding opponents. Darin Harvey was soon brought on to handle the business side of her career.

Before her first fight, there was one battle in particular that Rousey would need to have with a very familiar foe: her mother. The initial conversation between mother and daughter didn't go well, with De Mars vehemently opposing Rousey's MMA aspirations. De Mars was focused on a long-term plan for Rousey and repeatedly reminded her that women were barely part of the MMA landscape at the time.

A few weeks later, Rousey invited her mother to dinner, where they were joined by Harvey and Leo Frincu, her strength and conditioning coach. The two men did their best to sell De Mars on the plan, but she was still skeptical. De Mars called Rousey later that night. While not completely sold on the idea, she uttered two words that gave Rousey hope: "One year."

Rousey had finally received the approval she wanted most. It was time to go full speed ahead. She began working with trainer Edmond Tarverdyan at the Glendale Fighting Club. In addition, she had three part-time jobs—overnights at a fitness club, teaching judo at a club on the west side of Los Angeles, and as a vet assistant at an animal rehab clinic. Rousey's MMA training became part of a frenetic daily routine that included juggling the three jobs to help pay her mounting bills, as she explained in an interview with *Esquire* magazine on November 10, 2015.

> Even if nobody believed me, I believed it. I felt so happy every day, even though I was hustling and driving in the Honda with no AC, and going to three or four workouts a day and working three different jobs, and I was so happy and alive and so convinced that everything I was doing was right. Every single day that I lay down and collapsed in the bed, I was so convinced that that sleep was really earned and every

spare moment that I had, every spare thought was for fighting. I was shadowboxing with the droplets in the shower, just trying to get better every single second.

The biggest hurdle early on was finding an opponent. Harvey would comb the region looking for a fight, but any qualified fighters weren't too eager to go toe-to-toe with a judo champion who trained regularly with men. Rousey's reputation had preceded her.

The Dream Begins

Rousey made her amateur MMA debut on August 6, 2010, in a promotion called the Combat Fight League. She took on kickboxer Hayden Munoz. The setting was a club in Oxnard, California, about thirty miles (48 km) west of downtown Los Angeles. Rousey put Munoz down with her signature **armbar** submission just twenty-three seconds into the first round. For Munoz, it would be her first and only MMA fight.

Despite the crowd being less than one hundred people, Rousey was overwhelmed by the result and response. She wrote in her autobiography:

> The referee called stop and suddenly the whole world came back into view. Only this time it was a better world. The crowd was cheering, screaming and whistling, and they were cheering for me. I raised my fist in the air, making a victory lap around the cage. I felt a level of joy that I had never experienced before. It wasn't merely the victory; the joy came from a place much deeper, from an understanding that this was only the beginning.

Rousey's next two fights were part of the Tuff-N-Uff 145-pound (66 kg) amateur women's tournament in Las Vegas. The Tuff-N-Uff series was founded in 1994 to help promote combat sports and lobby for sanctioning throughout the United States. The organization's first event took place on November 14, 2003, which was also the first amateur MMA event to be sanctioned by the state of Nevada.

In her second amateur bout on November 12, 2010, Rousey once again used her armbar to submit Autumn Richardson after just fifty-seven seconds to move on to the tournament semifinals. She had won only two amateur fights, but Rousey was starting to feel the career momentum beginning. So much so that she made comments about wanting to challenge the Strikeforce Women's Champion, Cristiane "Cyborg" Santos, before the end of 2011.

A former national team handball player from Brazil, Santos started her MMA career in 2005. She made her United States debut in July 2008 and captured the inaugural Strikeforce Women's title with a first-round TKO of Gina Carano on August 15, 2009. The fight was broadcast live on the Showtime network and marked the first time two women ever headlined a major MMA event. An estimated 856,000 viewers tuned into Showtime for the Carano/Santos fight, setting an MMA ratings record for the network.

Santos would defend her title on two occasions in 2010, with wins over Marlos Coenen and Jan Finney. Santos was named Female Fighter of the Year at the World MMA Awards in 2009 and 2010 and was recognized by *Sports Illustrated* as the Female Fighter of the Year in 2009.

Santos's career was derailed for one year when a third title defense over Hiroko Yamanaka on December 17, 2011 was overturned three weeks later because Santos tested positive for stanozolol, an anabolic steroid. Santos was fined $2,500 and also had her license suspended. Stanozolol is the same steroid that Canadian sprinter Ben Johnson tested positive for at the 1988 Summer Olympics after winning the gold medal.

Rousey put on another impressive and efficient display in her next fight when she defeated Taylor "No Mercy" Stratford on January 7, 2011, in the Tuff-N-Uff tournament semifinals. The win came just days after Santos's suspension was announced. Rousey only needed twenty-four seconds and an armbar submission to beat Stratford, who was the number one-ranked amateur female fighter in the United States at the time.

It had taken Rousey a grand total of 104 seconds to dispatch the first three opponents in her MMA career. These were bold statements to the entire MMA world by Rousey, displaying the dominance that she knew she was capable of. However, there would be no Tuff-N-Uff championship match. With three dominant amateur performances behind her, the undefeated Rousey decided it was time to turn pro.

Turning Pro

Turning pro wasn't an immediate life changer for Rousey. She was still working three part-time jobs while finding time to squeeze in her daily workouts. She understood the big picture of her dream; it just seemed to be taking longer than expected to come to fruition.

Brazilian fighter Ediane Gomes would be Rousey's first professional opponent. The two women were scheduled to go head-to-head at the "King of The Cage: Turning Point" event in Tarzana,

California, on March 27, 2011. Each woman would receive $400 for appearing, with the winner pocketing an additional $400.

But two days away from her highly-anticipated professional debut, Rousey's career nearly went to the dogs. Some indoor playtime between Rousey's dog, Mochi, and a friend's dog—a 60-pound (27 kg) pit bull—started to turn nasty. Mochi, an 80-pound (36 kg) Argentine mastiff, had grabbed the other dog by the neck and started to become increasingly violent. Sensing the situation was getting out of control, Rousey kicked Mochi in the ribs to free up the other dog. Mochi then bit Rousey on her shin and punctured her foot with another deep bite. The cut on her foot required six stitches on top and three on the arch to repair.

Despite the throbbing pain in her stitched and swollen foot, Rousey had devised a plan for the weigh-in on the day of the fight. In addition to the weigh-in, each fighter had to submit to a medical check. One problem: stitches weren't allowed by the California Athletic Commission.

Even though Gomes had come in at 4 pounds (1.8 kg) over the 145-pound (66 kg) limit, Rousey was determined to make the weight she'd worked so hard to maintain. As a way to distract the officials, Rousey said she was concerned about being over the weight limit, and asked to be weighed in naked—with her back to the crowd, shielded by a towel. In the commotion afterwards, Rousey was able to put her sock back on to avoid having anyone see her injured foot. On fight night, Rousey wore an upside-down ankle sleeve secured with duct tape to cover the stitched foot. The weigh-in shenanigans would take up more time than the actual fight, as Rousey submitted the highly-touted Gomes with an armbar twenty-five seconds into the first round. As she described the fight to the *Los Angeles Daily News*:

I knew I was going to win that fight quickly. When I came out to actually fight, I stomped my feet on the ground to prove to myself, you're fine. And I came out and did a jab and a left hook into a clinch. I tried to throw forward, she resisted and I swept her backwards and I swept her right on the arch of the foot where the stitches were. Swept her, went into a mount, got past mount, straight into an armbar … and that was it.

Recording her first professional win was a huge step, both mentally and physically, for Rousey. Defeating Gomes proved to the MMA world that she was capable of defeating a tough opponent. From a personal standpoint, being able to win the fight in such convincing fashion despite having an injured foot showed Rousey that she had the mental focus to overcome adversity.

Almost There

Next up for Rousey was a fight with Canadian Charmaine "Not So Sweet" Tweet in Calgary, Alberta on June 17, 2011, at the Hard Knocks Fighting Championship "School of Hard Knocks 12" event.

Even though the setting for the fight with Tweet wasn't ideal—it was held at a dingy casino in Alberta—the bout would turn out to be a winning proposition on many levels for Rousey. She won in her typical fashion, using an armbar submission at the forty-nine-second mark of the first round. The winner's payout of $1,000 was the biggest of her young career.

But the biggest news of all came after the fight, when Rousey's trainer informed her that she had received a contract offer to compete in Strikeforce. This would be a huge step in her career,

Rousey's Rival

Before Ronda Rousey came along, Miesha Tate was the dominant female in the ultimate fighting world. Tate wrestled for four years at Franklin Pierce High School in Tacoma, Washington. As the only female on the team, she had to work out with the boys. As a senior in 2005, she won the women's state high school championship.

Miesha Tate poses with UFC commissioner Dana White at the weigh-in prior to her bout with Amanda Nunes at UFC 200.

Tate accepted her first MMA amateur fight in March 2006 and went 5-1 overall before turning pro. She earned the Strikeforce women's bantamweight title in 2011.

She crossed career paths with Rousey several times, twice going head-to-head in the **octagon**. She has also done some modeling and acting in feature films. Rousey took away Tate's Strikeforce title in their first meeting on March 3, 2012, in Columbus, Ohio. She improved her record to 2-0 all-time against Tate with a third-round armbar submission in UFC 168 on December 28, 2013.

Tate rebounded from those defeats to beat several top UFC competitors and earn what she thought was another shot at Rousey. Instead, that fight went to Holly Holm, who beat Rousey in the second round by a technical knockout.

Tate was then given the chance to fight Holm, and she took the champion's belt on March 6, 2016. Tate never got another chance at revenge with Rousey. She lost to Amanda Nunes on July 9, 2016, and to Raquel Pennington on November 12 of that year. After that, she retired. At the age of thirty, she said she no longer had the desire to fight.

"I have been in contact sports over half my life," she told MMAWeekly.com. "It doesn't have the same thrill that it did when I was twenty-two. I won't go in there and fight with half a heart."

as Strikeforce was the most legitimate MMA organization to offer a highly-competitive women's division. They'd already made household names out of women like Gina Carano and Miesha Tate.

Strikeforce started in 1985 primarily as a kickboxing organization. In its heyday, Strikeforce had television deals with CBS and Showtime, providing national exposure to a sport that still wasn't considered part of the mainstream. Many considered Strikeforce to be a second tier to UFC, but several fighters eventually moved over to UFC and became champions in their respective divisions. In March of 2011, Strikeforce was purchased by Zuffa, the parent company of UFC. The last Strikeforce show took place on March 12, 2013.

"My life was going to radically change," Rousey wrote in her autobiography. "I was going to be able to quit all of my other jobs and support myself as a fighter. I was going to prove all of the people who said I shouldn't be a fighter wrong. I was going to have enough money to fix my car windows and maybe even the air conditioning. I might even be able to afford to move to a nicer place."

Strikeforce Debut

Rousey's Strikeforce debut would come quickly, with Sarah D'Alelio providing the opposition in Las Vegas on August 12, 2011. With her focus now 100 percent on MMA, Rousey and her team created a four-week training camp to guarantee she'd be in peak physical condition for the fight.

Even with it now being a grander stage, the script for this fight was no different than the previous five of Rousey's career: attack quickly and engage the armbar for a submission victory. It was all over in twenty-five seconds, but this win—for which she would receive $8,000— would come with some controversy. Rousey went back to her judo training to lock in a flying armbar on D'Alelio, rendering her other arm useless. D'Alelio called out as they fell to the ground, prompting what's known as a "verbal tap" or a verbal submission. The end of the fight was greeted by strong objections from the fans in attendance, who couldn't hear D'Alelio call out to the referee.

"I could feel her arm going to catch herself and I knew the second her hand hit the ground, my weight would go through her arm and her arm would be obliterated," Rousey said to the LA Daily News. "And as she was falling, she was yelling 'Tap! Tap! Tap! Tap!' So as her hand hit the ground, I let my legs fall off as her hand hit the ground to not break her arm, then I recaught my position."

Rousey left no doubt in her next Strikeforce fight, using the armbar to dislocate Julia Budd's elbow for a thirty-nine-second win on November 18, 2011. This appeared to set up a bout with Sarah Kaufman, leaving Rousey one step away from taking on Miesha Tate for a shot at the women's championship.

That's when the Strikeforce matchmaker stepped in, granting Rousey the next shot at Tate. Despite Tate's immediate objections to the decision, the championship fight was set for March 3, 2012, at Nationwide Arena in Columbus, Ohio. Rousey and Tate were scheduled to be the second-last match of the night, behind the main event final of the Heavyweight Grand Prix between Josh Barnett and Daniel Cormier.

Tate was the reigning women's bantamweight champion and carried a record of 12-2 into the match. The upstart Rousey was

Rousey attempts to lock up Miesha Tate in a submission hold during their Strikeforce title fight on March 3, 2012 in Columbus, Ohio.

4-0, with all four wins coming via submission in the first minute of each fight.

The buildup to the fight was nothing Rousey had ever experienced before. Interspersed with Rousey's training camp regimen were regular media appearances and interviews. The two women were often interviewed together, and it was clear they didn't like each other. Tate felt like Rousey was an upstart coming after her title, while Rousey believed that Tate didn't respect her talent and Olympic pedigree.

Ronda Rousey: Conquering New Ground

An injury to Cormier cancelled the finals of the Heavyweight Grand Prix, vaulting the Rousey-Tate fight to headliner status. The trash-talking between the pair in the weeks leading up to the event just added to the anticipation of the title match, with both women expressing their disdain for the other. It was the first time that women would headline a card since Carano-Santos in 2009.

Rousey expected a battle from Tate, and that's how it played out. The two reached a milestone early, as Tate became the first fighter to last beyond the one-minute mark with Rousey. Rousey made an early attempt at an armbar submission, but the veteran Tate fought

It was sweet relief for Ronda Rousey after she defeated Miesha Tate to become the new Strikeforce women's bantamweight champion.

her way out of it. The two would continue battling, with Rousey holding a decisive edge. Rousey won the fight in the first round. As the clock ticked down, Rousey locked in the armbar and dislocated Tate's elbow. The champion had no choice but to tap out. The end came at the 4:27 mark, making it the longest fight of Rousey's young career.

"(Tate) is much more savvy on the ground than I anticipated," Rousey told reporters after the fight. "She's good, she's legit. But I don't feel too bad about it [hurting her arm]."

"It's a little sore, but I came here to put on a fight," Tate said. "I really didn't like her so I wanted to come out hard. I got a little overzealous, and she caught the arm."

When the championship belt was presented to Rousey, she recalled the wave of emotions that came over her.

"I felt relief, then I was overwhelmed by indescribable joy. I stood in the middle of the cage as the announcer called out, 'Ladies and gentlemen, we have a time of four minutes and 27 seconds in round number one. She is the winner by submission. She is still undefeated. She is the new Strikeforce women's world bantamweight champion. Rowdy Ronda Rousey.'"

For less than five minutes of work that night, Rousey took home a check totaling $32,000. Ronda Rousey, the new women's champion, had finally arrived.

Chapter 4

Famous Last Words

It was late on the night on January 19, 2011, and UFC Commissioner Dana White was leaving a posh restaurant in downtown Beverly Hills. Waiting outside the restaurant was a cameraman for TMZ.com, the tabloid news outlet that specializes in juicy quotes and salacious photos. On this night, the often bombastic and outspoken White would give them exactly what they came for.

"When are we going to see women in the UFC?" asked the TMZ cameraman.

"Never," replied White with a laugh. "Never."

White's biggest fear in adding a women's division to UFC was the lack of elite talent and competition. He'd seen female fights in other companies and had never been overly impressed. White had built an empire in UFC featuring incredibly talented male fighters that could also deliver when it came to self-promotion. He believed that simply adding women to a pay-per-view event would result in a boring fight that would upset the paying customers. This was a gamble he wasn't ready to take.

Opposite: UFC Commissioner Dana White is the sport's most powerful figure, but there was a time when he wanted no part of a woman fighting in his organization.

More than a year after White gave his infamous answer, Rousey was giving him pause. The former Olympic judoka was unbeaten in three professional fights and three others as an amateur. When Rousey captured the Strikeforce women's championship over Miesha Tate in March, the headline event had an average audience of 431,000 on the Showtime cable network.

Rousey defended her Strikeforce title for the first time on August 18, 2012 against Sarah Kaufman at the Valley View Casino Center in San Diego. This would be Kaufman's first shot at Rousey after she was passed over for the chance to take on Tate in March's championship fight.

There was also a special guest sitting ringside for the night: Dana White. As Rousey delivered her signature armbar submission fifty-four seconds into the first round that night in San Diego, Kaufman tapped out in full view of White. The irony of the moment wasn't lost on Rousey, "I actually forced her posture straight, so I finished it from the bottom right in front of Dana," Rousey told the *Daily News*. "He came to that fight himself, and it was literally like, I finished the armbar upside down and facing him—like, that's for you."

The attendance may have topped out at just over 3,500, but the Showtime viewership increased 23 percent from the Tate fight to a peak of 676,000 viewers. Not only was it the most-watched Strikeforce event of the year, it also drew the largest male 18–49 audience since February 2011.

Cover Girl

Even without the UFC brand attached to her name, Rousey was starting to develop the crossover success that most athletes can only dream of. Prior to the Kaufman fight, Rousey was photographed by *ESPN the Magazine* to appear in its annual Body Issue. Much to her surprise, Rousey was selected to appear on the cover.

The Body Issue is an annual collection of artistic photographs featuring athletes from all over the world in nude or semi-nude poses. Joining Rousey in the 2012 Body Issue were US women's soccer legend Abby Wambach, NCAA and WNBA standout Candace Parker, the NFL's Rob Gronkowski and Maurice Jones-Drew, and Slovakian tennis star Daniela Hantuchova.

Six MMA fighters have appeared in the pages of this special edition of the magazine: Rousey, Conor McGregor, Miesha Tate, Jon Jones, Cristiane Justino (Santos), and her former husband, Evangelista "Cyborg" Santos, from whom she had borrowed her nickname. Of the group, Rousey is the only one to appear on the magazine's cover.

The Meeting

Three weeks after taking in Rousey's title defense in San Diego, White contacted her. He was going to be in Beverly Hills for the *Sons of Anarchy* (television show) premiere in a couple of days, and he wanted Rousey to join him for dinner prior.

Rousey got dressed up and drove her beat-up Honda to White's hotel. From there she was taken by White's personal driver to Mr. Chow, a world-famous Chinese restaurant in the heart of Beverly Hills, long considered a staple by some of Hollywood's biggest stars and power brokers.

Early into the meal, White explained the significance of their dinner location. Not only was this his favorite restaurant, it was also the place where White made his famous statement about not having women in the UFC. Then White told Rousey something that would change her life.

"I brought you here tonight to tell you that you're going to be the first woman in the UFC."

A stunned Rousey didn't know how to react. This had been her dream for years, and in the blink of an eye it had become reality. The one person who controlled the decision, the same one who openly stated that women would never compete in the UFC, had just told her that she was going to be a groundbreaker. However, history would have to wait. Rousey was sworn to secrecy while White worked out some business details. The only person she confided in was Tarverdyan. She didn't even share the news with her business manager.

White told Rousey that not only would she be the first woman in the UFC, but she would also immediately carry the title as the women's champion. Rousey reluctantly declined that part of the offer, stating that she didn't feel comfortable being anointed the champion with a belt without first competing in a fight.

White held firm with his decision, explaining that this is how they'd done it in the past with the men. When introducing a new division, they immediately name a champion as well. Rousey officially signed her contract with UFC in November, but the delay in announcing the news was because of UFC's negotiations with the Showtime cable network and the impending shutdown of the Strikeforce organization.

Welcome to the Show

Following weeks of speculation and several false alarms, Rousey was finally introduced to the media by White at a press conference

A beaming Rousey shows off her championship belt, after being unveiled as the new UFC women's bantamweight champion at a press conference in Seattle on December 6, 2012.

in Seattle on December 6, 2012. The historic announcement came at the conclusion of the press conference that was part of the pre-event promotion for the UFC card two nights later featuring Benson Henderson and Nate Diaz at the KeyArena.

As he promised, White awarded Rousey a UFC championship belt and announced that she would defend it in the main event of UFC 157 against Liz Carmouche on February 23, 2013, in Anaheim, California.

"It means a lot," Rousey told reporters. "I feel like we have a lot to prove at this event, and no one's going to be disappointed. The women are here to stay, and we're gonna prove it."

Many people were surprised that Cristiane "Cyborg" Santos wasn't going to be Rousey's first UFC opponent. In answering why that wasn't the case, Rousey's trademark bravado shined through.

"It's going to happen eventually," Rousey said. "I can't make these girls fight me when I want them to fight me, and I have a lot of respect for Liz. She was the only one that really stepped up and said she wanted this fight right now. It speaks a lot to her. When the other girls want to come around and come into the big show, they know where I'm at."

White could only stand back and smile as Rousey dealt with her first real media scrum. In many ways, Rousey validated his reasons for signing her to the UFC while alleviating any fears he might have had.

"She speaks well; the media loves her. It's hard not to like her," White said. "But some people don't like her, don't like the way she talks. But regardless of what you think about her personality, she's a mean, nasty fighter and that's what I look for and that's what I care about."

The Ultimate Debut

Rousey's UFC debut would take place at the Honda Center in Anaheim, California, the home of the National Hockey League's Anaheim Ducks. It's a palatial Orange County venue surrounded by palm trees, and its concourses are lined with marble and granite imported from around the world. This was a long way from the casino back rooms and dirty, small-town gyms in which Rousey's fights had been staged.

The milestone Rousey–Carmouche fight was the main event of a twelve-fight card featuring popular UFC stars Urijah Faber, Dan Henderson, and Robbie Lawler. Rousey's payout for the night was $45,000, and Carmouche received $12,000. The winner would get an additional $45,000.

From the moment Rousey's first UFC fight was announced in December, the momentum built as the date got closer. UFC officials said the media circus surrounding the fight was like nothing they'd ever seen. Rousey spent a significant amount of time doing interviews in the weeks leading in. Her normally early wake-up calls got even earlier and quite often involved some form of interview or live television appearance. The media feeding frenzy included nonsporting outlets such as *Rolling Stone*, CNN and *Forbes*, along with coverage from ESPN and the various MMA outlets that normally covered UFC events.

"No fighter has ever fought in the UFC that has had more attention than she has," White said. "It's a fact. Honestly, going into it, I didn't know that would happen. I didn't know HBO and *Time* magazine and all these other outlets that never cover us would."

The decision to make Carmouche the first opponent for Rousey was questioned by many, but she was definitely worthy of the opportunity. She came into the fight with a record of 7-2 and had won her last two fights. Carmouche had also spent five years serving with the US Marine Corps, working as an aviation electrician while doing three tours of duty in the Middle East.

And while Rousey was breaking barriers as the first UFC women's champion, Carmouche was making news of her own. Not only was she the second woman signed to a UFC contract, Carmouche became the organization's first openly gay fighter. Carmouche served in the Marines under the US government's "Don't Ask Don't Tell" policy— the US government policy prohibiting gays, lesbians, and bisexuals from living openly while serving in the military—but said her UFC experiences couldn't have been any more welcoming on all levels.

Fight Night

"Everything I had dreamed about and everything I had worked for was on the verge of coming true. But I also knew that if I didn't win, it all would have been for nothing," Rousey stated in her autobiography.

The fight was a battle from the moment the opening bell rang. Adrenaline got to Rousey early, and Carmouche's ground-and-pound style was nothing she had experienced before. Rousey knew Carmouche was strong, and the former Marine used that strength to engage Rousey in a rear-naked **choke hold** that turned into a violent neck crank. This was a move that Rousey had never experienced before in MMA or judo, and it dislocated her jaw. Her lower teeth

Liz Carmouche (*top*) gave Rousey everything she could handle in their historic bantamweight championship fight at UFC 157 on February 23, 2013 in Anaheim.

cut halfway into her upper lip, while her top teeth were digging into Carmouche's arm.

Rousey was finally able to pry Carmouche's legs off of her and tossed her to the mat. It was there that she let her primal instincts kick in. With just eleven seconds left in the opening round, Rousey was able to take control and locked in the armbar for the submission victory at 4:49 of the first round in a scheduled three-round fight.

There would be no disputing it now. Rousey wasn't a paper champion, or one that had simply been anointed by the UFC Commissioner. Any uncomfortable feelings that she had about simply being named the champion had disappeared. The first women's champion in the history of UFC had endured the longest fight of her life and was now able to proudly hold the title belt high above her head without any hesitation.

The historic night was witnessed by an arena crowd of 15,525, and more than 500,000 viewers purchased the pay-per-view telecast at home for a fee of $49.99.

The Fight She Never Saw Coming

Another sign of Rousey's rise to fame was her involvement as a coach in season eighteen of *The Ultimate Fighter*, a reality TV show in which sixteen MMA contestants live together in Las Vegas and compete against each other for the goal of winning a UFC contract. Past coaches have included MMA stars such as Ken Shamrock, Chuck Liddell, Quinton Jackson, and Randy Couture.

The show was initially created by the UFC to help drive their product to the mainstream using cable TV. *TUF* debuted in 2005 on Spike TV, where it ran until 2011. It moved to FX for 2012–2013, and has aired on Fox Sports 1 since September 2013.

As Rousey's legend grew, so did the demands on her time. Walking the red carpet and attending galas became the norm for the budding superstar.

Social Media Support

When Rousey faced Bethe Correia at UFC 190 on August 1, 2015 in Brazil, the Twitterverse was abuzz with support for the reigning UFC women's champion. From athletes to actors to musicians, they were all in awe when Rousey needed just thirty-four seconds for the devastating knockout win.

Some tweeted words of encouragement before the fight.

Good luck to @RondaRousey!! #ShesABeast #StriveForGreatness —NBA star LeBron James

Always got my girl RR's back. Both undefeated. Huge fight! #ItsShowtime #AndSTILL #UFC190 —actor and former professional wrestler Dwayne "The Rock" Johnson

Good luck to the champ @RondaRousey #UFC190 —singer Nick Jonas

Let's goooo @RondaRousey ! #winbabywin #UFC @ufc #rouseyvscorreia —actor Jerry Ferrara

Can't wait to see @RondaRousey defend her title tonight. Should be a killer night in #Brazil HERE WE GO! —actor Chris Pratt

Others just couldn't wait to express themselves after the quick win.

Ronda Rousey is the Greatest Champion of this era! Keep Punching CHAMP! —actor Sylvester Stallone

Ronda Rousey is a beast Daaaaaaaaaamn —Former NBA all-star Shaquille O'Neal

That's how you #shhhhhh #UFC190 #nomercy —NFL quarterback Aaron Rodgers

Huge congrats to @RondaRousey!! Can't wait for our next fight. —actor Mark Wahlberg

Wow. That was @CarliLloyd against Japan fast! Skills demonstrated. Congrats @RondaRousey! #StillTheChamp —soccer player Hope Solo

That moment you want to settle in and watch @RondaRousey but you blink and she already destroyed that chick. Haha —actress Ruby Rose

THAT'S MY GIRL!!!!!!!!!!!!! @RondaRousey #UFC190 —singer Demi Lovato

Ronda Rousey=The End! —singer Chris Daughtry

A focused Rousey locks eyes with her nemesis Miesha Tate at the weigh-in prior to their much-anticipated title fight at UFC 168 in Las Vegas.

Ronda Rousey: Conquering New Ground

Adding Rousey as a coach was another sign the UFC wanted to increase her exposure, while also following up on White's commitment to expand the women's division. For the first time ever, season eighteen featured eight men and eight women competing for two separate UFC contracts. It was also the first time the show would feature a pair of female coaches, and the two coaches would square off as part of an upcoming pay-per-view event. This element of the show would also turn into a career-defining moment for Rousey.

During the show's first episode, Rousey was blindsided by the appearance of her rival, Miesha Tate, as the opposing coach. Rousey went into the series fully expecting to see Cat Zingano walk through the door. In full view of the cameras, a visibly upset Rousey demanded to talk with White about the unannounced change in coaches.

Even though White assured her the late change was precipitated by an injury to Zingano, Rousey believed it had more to do with a comment made to White from her manager demanding more money for taking part in that season. In Rousey's mind, White was making an example of her.

This immediate drama made for great reality television and gave people a different perception of Rousey's "golden girl" personality. Thanks to the show's editors, Rousey and Tate were shown to clash at every turn throughout, sometimes in petty fashion. This became a "**heel turn**" moment for the former Olympian, who was often portrayed as petulant and whiny throughout the season.

When the women fought at UFC 168 (December 28, 2013), it turned into an all-out war for Rousey. It had been six months since filming ended, but the champ had a long memory of what Tate did to her during the series.

The fight would last into the third round for the first—and only—time in her career, and Rousey took advantage of every second she had inside the octagon that night with Tate. Rousey ended the fight with an armbar submission. She described her strategy in her autobiography:

> Afterward, there were people who thought she challenged me in that fight, because it went into the third round. But I had dragged that fight out intentionally, wanting to punish Miesha for as long as I possibly could. When I had thoroughly defeated her, when I had crushed her all the way down to the bottom of her soul, then I went for the armbar. Miesha was beat and exhausted. I had never felt better in my life.

Looking to the Future

While rocketing to stardom in the UFC, Rousey started giving thought to her career beyond fighting. She was the first to admit that life in the UFC wasn't going to last forever, and it was time to start thinking about her future. One thing that had always interested her was movies.

Whenever Rousey gave thought to becoming a crossover star, the name Gina Carano would always come into her head. Carano started in MMA in 2006 and built a career record of 7-1. Her only loss came to Cristiane "Cyborg" Santos in her final fight on August 15, 2009. Carano had some small TV and film roles early in her career before

Former MMA fighter Gina Carano is considered the trailblazer for crossover success, transitioning from the octagon to a film career in Hollywood.

being cast as the lead by famed director Steven Soderbergh in the spy thriller *Haywire* in 2009. Carano also costarred in *Fast & Furious 6* and appeared in *Deadpool* in the role of Angel Dust.

Rousey signed with the William Morris Endeavor (WME-IMG) agency and began taking meetings with producers and studio executives. WME-IMG is a Beverly Hills-based talent and marketing agency that specializes in entertainment, sports, and fashion. In July 2016, WME-IMG purchased UFC from Zuffa for a record-setting $4 billion.

Hollywood icon Sylvester Stallone tabbed Rousey for her first big screen role in the action-film, *The Expendables 3*. The movie was shot in Bulgaria while Rousey trained for UFC 168.

One producer who took an immediate interest in Rousey was the legendary Sylvester Stallone. He was casting for *The Expendables 3* movie and thought Rousey would be perfect for the role of Luna, a nightclub bouncer. Stallone wrote and produced *The Expendables* and wrote the next two films in the series, which pay tribute to the great action blockbusters of the 1980s and 1990s, and feature stars like Arnold Schwarzenegger, Chuck Norris, and Dolph Lundgren.

The two had their first meeting prior to Rousey leaving to shoot *The Ultimate Fighter* in Las Vegas, and they would meet on two more occasions when she returned. Rousey was eventually offered the part and spent eight weeks on set in Bulgaria.

One challenge Rousey faced during filming was keeping up her training regimen, as she was preparing to fight Tate in UFC 168. Many days on set would last sixteen hours, and the role was very physically demanding. Rousey found a gym to work out in each day with boxer Victor Ortiz, who was also part of the cast. She was even able to recruit some Bulgarian wrestlers to keep her grappling skills fresh, although their skills weren't up to her standards.

Upon returning to the United States, Rousey went straight to Atlanta, where she spent ten days in November filming *Furious 7*, the seventh installment of the *The Fast and the Furious* franchise that starred Vin Diesel, Dwayne "The Rock" Johnson, and the late Paul Walker. This would be another physical role for Rousey, acting as the Head of Security for a billionaire in Abu Dhabi.

Chapter 5

A Model for Hope

After winning a bronze medal at the 2008 Olympics, Rousey began having dreams of a career in MMA. She had nothing to aspire to because such options weren't available to women, but this wasn't just about her. Rousey felt that if she could succeed in another sport beyond judo, she'd be guiding the way for those after her and giving them hope that there was more to look forward to.

In four short years, Rousey achieved that and more. Rousey didn't just break down the door to the UFC in 2012, she kicked it down and marched through triumphantly. While others before her had achieved athletic success, they were unable to truly capitalize on their fame as Rousey has done.

While the result wasn't what she hoped for, Rousey's knockout loss in the second round to Holly Holm at UFC 193 on November 14, 2015, has become the benchmark for UFC women's events. A record crowd of 57,240 packed Etihad Stadium in Melbourne,

Opposite: Ronda Rousey defeated Serena Williams and Lindsey Vonn to be named the Best Female Athlete at the 2015 ESPY Awards in Los Angeles.

Australia, to watch a UFC event featuring four women at the top of the card.

Rousey and Holm were the main event, with a Women's Strawweight Championship fight between Joanna Jędrzejczyk and Valérie Létourneau listed as the co-main event. The 1.1 million pay-per-view purchases also marked the highest total for Rousey's five UFC headline bouts.

After more than a year off following her only professional loss, Rousey returned to the octagon in UFC 207 on December 30, 2016, for one of the most anticipated events in sports. Rousey took on Amanda Nunes at T-Mobile Arena in Las Vegas, looking to reclaim the UFC Bantamweight championship that Holm took from her last year. For the fight, Rousey was paid $3 million, and Nunes $200,000, according to MMA.

The fight didn't go well for Rousey. Nunes punished her so badly the referee stopped the bout before it was a minute old. Afterward, Nunes said it was time for Rousey to retire, and UFC Commissioner Dana White went on ESPN and said he was uncertain she would ever fight again.

If the fight was her last, Rousey will be remembered as the one who, as ESPN's Phil Murphy said, "shattered the MMA's glass ceiling" and made it possible for participants such as Paige VanZant to be offered a spot on *Dancing With the Stars*. She has allowed other fighters to earn a lot of money.

White was the one responsible for bringing Rousey into UFC, and after her second loss he told ESPN how much she meant to him and to the sport:

> I went in there and hugged her for 45 minutes. I told her, 'I love you so much, and whatever you want to do

After more than a year off, Ronda Rousey was dispatched in the first round by Amanda Nunes at UFC 207 in Las Vegas on December 30, 2016.

next, I got your back. You built this. This doesn't exist without you. You're the best decision I ever made.' I walked out of the arena and people were crying, men and women. She has been an amazing role model and amazing partner, an amazing friend. For the millions of people who admire her, she is somebody who is actually worth the admiration. Believe me, there's a lot of celebrities out there that are popular. I meet them all the time. They are not worth your admiration. ... But Ronda Rousey is all of that. She's incredible.

Ronda Rousey Scorecard

Accomplishments

Judo: Won two United States Judo Association junior championships and won a gold and a bronze in under-20 world competition. Won six USJA senior championships and three gold, one silver, and one bronze medal at the Pan American judo championships. Won sixteen gold medals, two silver, and three bronze in international tournaments. Won a silver medal at the 2007 World Championships. Earned a bronze medal at the 2008 Summer Olympics.

MMA: Strikeforce Women's Champion, 2012; UFC Women's Bantamweight Champion, 2013–2015.

Awards

World MMA Female Fighter of the Year (2012, 2013, 2014); Yahoo! Sports Female Fighter of the Year and Breakthrough Fighter of the Year (2013); ESPY Award Best Female Athlete (2014, 2015) and Best Female Fighter (2015); Associated Press Female Athlete of the Year, third place (2015); *Sports Illustrated* Sportsman of the Year finalist (2015).

Rousey blazed a trail for women wanting to compete in the UFC, and her success in films and television made her one of the most recognizable and marketable women in the world.

By the young age of thirty, Rousey had opened the door for women in UFC and used her crossover success and worldwide platform to become one of the most polarizing figures in sports, one that empowers women of all ages.

Coming to Grips with Body Image

The most prominent issue that Rousey has dealt with throughout her life is body image and how it related to maintaining her fighting weight during her judo career. It even struck her early on as her body started to develop. Despite living in the heat and sun of Southern California, Rousey would wear nothing but baggy sweatpants and hoodies to cover the muscular, toned body that had become a source of embarrassment.

As Rousey struggled to make weight limits for judo tournaments, she would frequently find herself going days without food, surviving only on water and coffee. She couldn't enjoy food because everything she ate was scrutinized by those around her. It wasn't until years later that Rousey realized she had been dealing with **bulimia**, an eating disorder related to self-esteem over body image, usually involving self-induced vomiting after meals to prevent the possibility of any weight gain.

Rousey was the cover girl for *ESPN the Magazine's* Body Issue in 2012, and has also been featured on the cover of the *Sports Illustrated* swimsuit issue, *Maxim, Men's Fitness Australia,* and *Self.* Rousey has finally found a way to embrace the body that used to embarrass her.

"If I can represent that body type of women that isn't represented so much in media, then I'd be happy to do that," she told the *New York Times*. "When women say that going on publications directed at men is somehow demeaning, I don't think that's true. I think that's one really effective way to change the societal standard women are held to."

In 2013, Rousey hosted an event called "Don't Throw Up, Throw Down," raising $11,800 for Didi Hirsch Mental Health Services, a Southern California-based organization that provides counseling and mental health services, while working extensively with women dealing with body image issues.

The Didi Hirsch organization has also been the beneficiary of Rousey's "D.N.B." campaign. Rousey created a limited-edition T-shirt featuring the mantra that encourages women to take charge of their lives instead of letting others do it for them. Since launching the campaign in 2015, more than 56,000 T-shirts have been sold for $24.99, with a portion of the proceeds going to Didi Hirsch Mental Health Services.

Rousey has also appeared in ads for Buffalo Jeans and provided her expertise for a new line of their clothing. Not only was Rousey brought on to be the face of its brand in 2016, they gave her the opportunity to help design jeans that properly fit women with an athletic build. The "Hope" line of jeans come in sizes 25 to 34 with wider waistbands and more leg room and are made in a range of cuts including cropped skinny jeans, patterned boot-cut jeans, and a classic black straight-leg.

Having battled body image issues throughout her life, Rousey partnered with Buffalo Jeans to design a new line of jeans to properly fit athletic women.

A Charitable Heart

Prior to her 2015 fight against Bethe Correia in Brazil, Rousey donated $30,000 to a local program run by 2004 Olympic bronze medalist Flavio Canto, which promotes human development and social inclusion through sports and education, promoting judo from the initiation to the sport to a level of high performance.

Online auctions on rondarousey.net regularly feature unique items or autographed merchandise that fans can bid on to raise money for charities. For example, the fight-worn hand wraps from her UFC 190 match with Correia went for $3,050, with the proceeds going to an organization called the Lighthouse Preschool program.

Rousey has also run a Free Rice Campaign before each title fight to help raise food for the hungry. The campaign is run through FreeRice.com, a not-for-profit organization that supports the United Nations World Food Programme. For every question answered correctly on the website during the campaign, ten grains of rice are donated by the sponsor. In her first six UFC fights, Rousey's campaign helped donate 278 million grains of rice, which would feed 81,765 people.

In 2009, Rousey started Gompers Judo, an inner-city judo program run out of the Gompers Middle School in Los Angeles where her sister, Jennifer, used to be a student teacher. The goal of the program is to enrich the lives of kids through judo, while giving them the opportunity to become part of a team.

Money Talks

Of the ten highest-paid female athletes in 2016 (a period from June 2015 to June 2016), Rousey ranked third overall behind tennis stars Serena Williams ($28.9 million) and Maria Sharapova ($23.8 million). Rousey earned a total of $14 million during this time, including $10 million in purses and bonuses for her two UFC fights with Holm and Correia. This was a jump of five spots from 2015 for Rousey, when she totaled earnings of $6.5 million.

From a marketing standpoint, Rousey's brand awareness of 66 percent is the fourth-highest among female athletes behind the Williams sisters and NASCAR driver Danica Patrick.

Her corporate appeal continues to grow, and currently includes endorsement deals with Reebok, Buffalo Jeans, MetroPCS, Bud Light, Monster Energy, Fanatics, and EA Sports. Rousey and Conor McGregor appeared together on the cover of EA Sports' UFC 2 video game released in March 2016.

Charting the Course

Moving from judo to MMA wasn't done immediately by Rousey, but over time she realized that it was a natural progression that could pave the way for others down the road. The first woman to benefit from this could be twenty-six-year-old Kayla Harrison, a two-time Olympic judo gold medalist for the United States.

Harrison won gold at the 2012 and 2016 Olympics in the 78-kg (172 pound) class and also captured gold at the 2011 and 2015 Pan American Championships. Her career path closely mirrors Rousey's, and she's aware of the possibilities that lie ahead.

"It's an opportunity that I didn't have five years, six years ago," said Harrison, who has trained with Rousey on several occasions. "For me, it'd be dumb of me not to consider it. I have an opportunity to make a lot of money and do something that could potentially be a lot of fun."

Kayla Harrison won a gold medal for the United States in women's judo at the 2016 Summer Olympics, and she is already considering following in Ronda Rousey's footsteps.

Silver Screen Success

Looking to a career beyond UFC, Rousey hired a talent agent and began taking acting lessons to make herself a viable commodity to movie producers. Rousey made her big screen debut in *The Expendables 3* in 2014. That was followed by her role as Luna in *Furious 7*, in which she battled actress Michelle Rodriguez in an epic fight scene.

Rousey moved away from the action genre and was able to add a comedic role to her resume when she played herself in the *Entourage* movie, a big-screen version of the HBO series that ran for eight seasons. The storyline involved Rousey being pursued romantically by Turtle (Jerry Ferrara).

With numerous high-profile film roles already to her credit, Rousey has several projects coming up, including a collaboration with Tina Fey.

Next up for Rousey is a major starring role in the reboot of the cult classic *Road House*. Rousey will add a female twist to the role made famous by the late Patrick Swayze in 1989. Swayze starred as a bouncer hired to clean up one of the rowdiest bars in Missouri, while protecting the town from a corrupt businessman. Rousey is also set to star in the action film, *The Athena Project*. The film is an adaptation of Brad Thor's *New York Times* bestseller about an all-female commando team.

Writer and actress Tina Fey is a big fan of Rousey's, and the two are expected to be working together on a film in the next few years. The film originated from Rousey's "D.N.B." mantra and is expected to feature her as a no-nonsense instructor at a camp attended by wealthy, pampered wives.

Other film projects coming up for Rousey include the action film *Mile 22* with Mark Wahlberg and director Peter Berg, along with an adaptation of her 2015 best-selling biography, *My Fight/Your Fight*. That book was cowritten with her sister, Maria Burns Ortiz.

There's also some time on the small screen in Rousey's future. Rousey, Janet Jackson, and Serena Williams each signed a three-picture movie deal with the Lifetime cable network to bring stories that reflect their passions about empowerment to the screen.

Live from New York!

Rousey became just the third female athlete—and first in twenty-two years—to host *Saturday Night Live* when she did the honors on January 23, 2016, with musical guest Selena Gomez. The previous two were tennis legend Chris Evert on November 11, 1989, and figure-skating star Nancy Kerrigan on March 12, 1994.

Rousey's biography, *My Fight/Your Fight*, was released in 2015 and reached the *New York Times* best sellers list in June of that year.

A Model for Hope

Rousey appeared in several sketches throughout the show, including one where she got her revenge on the bullies at high school using her MMA skills. The episode drew a 5.0 rating and a 12 share, making it the fourth-most watched show of that season for *SNL*.

Wielding her Power

When MMA was finally legalized by New York State in April of 2016, Rousey was on hand for the press conference and took part in the ceremony when Governor Andrew Cuomo signed the bill.

New York was the last state in the country to legalize mixed martial arts, with lawmakers citing the sport's violent nature and insurance concerns as the reasons for the ban.

Rousey played an active role in getting MMA legalized in New York, making several trips to the state capitol building in Albany to

Ronda Rousey was active in campaigning for New York State to legalize MMA, and attended Governor Andrew Cuomo's press conference in April 2016.

discuss the bill in the months prior. The first MMA event to be held in New York since the legalization was UFC 205 at Madison Square Garden on November 12, 2016, with Conor McGregor defeating Eddie Alvarez in the main event. A boisterous crowd of 20,527 attended the event, and the gate receipts of $17.7 million were a UFC record. Even the weigh-in the day before attracted 15,000 fans to the Garden, and Rousey made a surprise appearance at the end to help promote her title match at UFC 207.

The Best of the Best

Rousey's impressive run of success in UFC has also carried over to a poll run by ESPNw in September of 2015. ESPNw is a subsection of ESPN.com that focuses primarily on women's sports. ESPNw's "Best Female Athlete" bracket challenge featured thirty-two of the best female athletes of all time, with the winners moving on to each round based on fan voting.

Rousey advanced to the final matchup, where she would eventually defeat the number one seed, Serena Williams, by earning 52 percent of the thirteen thousand votes that were cast in the final round. On her way to the matchup with Williams, Rousey defeated swimmer Missy Franklin, track and field legend Jackie Joyner-Kersee, basketball star Diana Taurasi, and Florence Griffith Joyner, who won three gold medals in track and field at the 1988 Olympics.

Williams advanced to the final round with wins over Cheryl Miller, the beach volleyball team of Kerri Walsh Jennings and Misty May-Treanor, multi-sport star Babe Didrikson Zaharias, and tennis powerhouse Steffi Graf.

Very Social Media

Building a brand takes time, and Rousey has done it very well through the use of social media. Rousey has more than 11 million followers on Facebook, 8.6 million on Instagram, and 3.2 million on Twitter. As a comparison, UFC men's champion Conor McGregor has 4.3 million Facebook followers and 7.4 million on Instagram.

She makes excellent use of Instagram, giving her fans exclusive behind-the-scenes photos from UFC events and the various other celebrity galas she regularly attends. Rousey also started the #RouseyRevolution campaign in 2015, encouraging her female fans to share their stories of toughness and empowerment through her various social media platforms.

Her online presence isn't just limited to social media. Rousey was ranked third overall by Google's annual list of the top trending people in 2015, recognizing the people recording the highest spikes in web traffic over a sustained period in 2015 as compared with 2014. Rousey trailed only Lamar Odom and Caitlyn Jenner, and finished one spot ahead of Donald Trump.

The Squared Circle

A future in movies may not be the only thing waiting for Rousey when her UFC career comes to an end. Rumors have persisted for years that the WWE (formerly the WWF) would be interested in having Rousey join them when she's done with MMA. Rousey would add an immediate spark to the WWE women's division that continues to grow in popularity, and she'd also be able to continue working film roles into her schedule as many of the WWE superstars do.

Rousey's life and career have been chronicled in the film, *Through My Father's Eyes: The Ronda Rousey Story*. Directed by Gary Stretch, the documentary was to be released in the spring of 2017.

A Model for Hope

Rousey made her surprise WWE debut at WrestleMania 31 in San Francisco, when she teamed up with The Rock to lay the smackdown on WWE executive Stephanie McMahon and her husband, Paul "Triple H" Levesque.

Rousey was sitting ringside when approached by The Rock (her *Furious 7* co-star) to get involved in the altercation he was having in the ring. She used a judo toss on Triple H before threatening to engage Stephanie in her deadly armbar. The appearance ended with The Rock triumphantly raising Rousey's hand in the ring.

The Influencer

When *Time* magazine came out with its list of the "100 Most Influential People" of 2016, Rousey was one of eleven sports figures on the list, joining the likes of Steph Curry, Usain Bolt, and Jordan Spieth. Each person was recognized with an essay written by someone famous. Actress Tina Fey penned the Rousey piece, saying the fighter sets an example for young girls with her fierce attitude and determination.

"Imagine if we could teach our daughters to value their bodies for what they can do, not for how others think they look," Fey wrote. "Could Ronda be the one to finally help us understand that as females, we define the word *feminine* and that it doesn't define us?"

Becoming BFFs with Ellen

When you becoming known for physically destroying your opponent, sometimes it's a good idea to display a softer side in the media to help win more fans. There's been no better platform for Rousey to do this than on her appearances on *The Ellen DeGeneres Show*, the Emmy Award-winning daytime talk and variety show.

Rousey has made three appearances on the show since September 2015, each time making headline news with a personal or professional revelation. Following her loss to Holly Holm, Rousey was incredibly emotional during a February 2016 appearance when she revealed that she'd had brief suicidal thoughts in the moments after the fight. The YouTube video of the interview has generated almost 6.8 million views since it aired.

During her third appearance in November 2016, Rousey told DeGeneres that her fight at UFC 207 might be one of her last, as she's considering winding down her career. There were more than 1.5 million views of this interview on YouTube in less than three weeks.

This goes to show that the once-anonymous judo Olympic medalist is now a role model for women whose words carry a lot of weight.

Timeline

February 1, 1987 Ronda Rousey is born in Glenview, California.

August 11, 1995 Ron Rousey, Ronda's father, commits suicide by asphyxiation.

July 7, 2002 Ronda Rousey wins United States Judo Association Juvenile C Championship, her first national title.

September 14, 2007 Wins silver medal representing the USA at the 2007 World Judo Championships in Brazil.

August 13, 2008 Wins bronze medal for USA in women's judo at the 2008 Summer Olympics in Beijing.

August 6, 2010 Makes amateur MMA debut vs. Hayden Munoz (first round, submission).

August 12, 2011 Defeats Sarah D'Alelio at Strikeforce (first round, submission).

November 18, 2011 Defeats Julia Budd at Strikeforce (first round, submission).

March 3, 2012 Defeats Miesha Tate at Strikeforce (first round, submission).

August 18, 2012 Defeats Sarah Kaufman at Strikeforce (first round, submission).

December 6, 2012 Dana White introduces Rousey as the first women's UFC champion.

February 23, 2013 Defeats Liz Carmouche at UFC 157 to defend her Women's Championship (first round, submission).

December 28, 2013 Defeats Miesha Tate at UFC 168 (third round, submission).

February 22, 2014 Defeats Sara McMann at UFC 170 (first round, TKO).

July 5, 2014 Defeats Alexis Davis at UFC 175 (first round, TKO).

February 28, 2015 Defeats Cat Zingano at UFC 184 (first round, submission)

August 1, 2015 Defeats Bethe Correia at UFC 190 (first round, TKO).

November 14, 2015 Loses to Holly Holm at UFC 193 (second round, TKO).

January 23, 2016 Hosts *Saturday Night Live* with musical guest Selena Gomez.

October 12, 2016 Announces return to UFC to fight Amanda Nunes at UFC 207.

December 30, 2016 Loses to Amanda Nunes at UFC 207 in Las Vegas (first round, TKO).

Glossary

apraxia A motor speech disorder caused by damage to the brain.

asphyxia A condition in which the body is deprived of oxygen. This causes unconsciousness and even death.

armbar A move in wrestling or judo that hyperextends the elbow or shoulder joint.

bulimia An eating disorder that uses methods such as vomiting to avoid weight gain.

choke hold Martial arts technique used to restrict an opponent's breathing.

heel turn When a person transforms from good to evil.

ippon A full point, the highest point that can be scored in Japanese martial arts, awarded for executing a technique perfectly.

judo A martial art that emphasizes quickness and the use of leverage to throw an opponent.

judoka Someone who practices judo, or is considered an expert in judo.

knockout When is fighter is knocked down and unconscious and can no longer defend himself or herself.

mixed martial arts An extreme combat sport in which participants may employ techniques used in boxing, wrestling, and various martial arts such as kickboxing, judo, and karate.

muay thai Combat sport that originated in Thailand, specializing in stand-up striking.

octagon The eight-sided UFC fighting area that measures 30 feet (9.1 m) across and 6 feet (1.8 m) high.

Olympic trials An event at which athletes compete for a spot on the US Olympic team.

Pan American Championships A now-annual event organized by the Panamerican Judo Confederation. The event was first held in Havana, Cuba, in 1952.

repechage A bracket featuring competitors who lost early in a competition, giving them a chance to move on to a medal round. The term is often used in rowing.

sensei A teacher, or instructor, of Japanese mixed martial arts, such as karate or judo.

submission When a fighter taps out (admits defeat) because they are locked in a hold and can no longer compete.

Summer Olympics International multisport event that takes place every four years.

Bibliography

Online Articles

Arth, Susie. "Ronda Rousey Tops Serena Williams, Voted Best Female Athlete Ever." ESPN.com. September 9, 2015 http://www.espn.com/espnw/news-commentary/article/13465064/best-female-athlete-ever-bracket

Bloody Elbow. "UFC 170: The Judo Career of Ronda Rousey." SB Nation. February 21, 2014. http://www.bloodyelbow.com/2014/2/21/5433290/ufc-170-the-judo-career-of-ronda-rousey

Gregory, Sean. "This Gold Medalist Could Be the Next Ronda Rousey." *Time.* August 15, 2016. http://time.com/4451726/kayla-harrison-mma-ronda-rousey-rio-2016-olympics-judo

Grinberg, Emanuella. "Why UFC 'Beast' Ronda Rousey is such a big deal." CNN. August 5, 2015. http://edition.cnn.com/2015/08/02/living/ronda-rousey-profile-feat

Huang, Mike. "Dana White on UFC 193: 'This Event Changed Everything'" ESPN.com. December 11, 2015. http://www.espn.com/espnw/newscommentary/article/14344107/dana-white-ufc-193-event-changed-everything

Maese, Rick. "How MMA found its feeder system in Olympic athletes." *Washington Post.* May 31, 2016. https://www.washingtonpost.com/sports/olympics/how-mma-found-its-feeder-system-in-olympic-athletes/2016/05/31/664c077e-2745-11e6-a3c4-0724e8e24f3f_story.html?utm_term=.549d4f93aa76

Majendie, Matt. "Newsmaker: Ronda Rousey." *The National.* August 6, 2015. http://www.thenational.ae/arts-lifestyle/profiles/newsmaker-ronda-rousey

Marikar, Sheila. "Ronda Rousey's Next Fight: Body Image in Hollywood." *New York Times.* October 9, 2015. https://www.nytimes.com/2015/10/11/fashion/ronda-rouseys-next-fight-body-image-in-hollywood.html?_r=0

Michaelis, Vicki. "Judo's former prodigy marshals her life, talents." *USA TODAY.* June 1, 2008. http://usatoday30.usatoday.com/sports/olympics/2008-06-01-rousey_n.htm

Mihoces, Gary. "Rousey's bronze makes U.S. history in women's judo." *USA TODAY.* August 13, 2008. http://usatoday30.usatoday.com/sports/olympics/beijing/fight/2008-08-13-womensjudo_n.htm

Pilon, Mary. "Caged: What Drives Ronda Rousey to Wake Up and Fight." *Esquire.* November 10, 2015, http://www.esquire.com/sports/a39499/ronda-rousey-esquire-1115

"Ronda Rousey, Down on Her Luck Judo Star Turned MMA Dominator." SB Nation.http://www.sbnation.com/sponsored/10634300/ronda-rousey-down-on-her-luck-judo-star-turned-mma-dominator

Sanneh, Kelefa. "Mean Girl." *New Yorker.* July 28, 2014. http://www.newyorker.com/magazine/2014/07/28/mean-girl

Shelburne, Ramona. "Rousey Says She's Down But Not Out." *ESPN The Magazine.* December 8, 2015. http://www.espn.com/espn/feature/story/_/page/espnwrousey/in-exclusive-interview-ronda-rousey-says-not-losing-holly-holm

Snowden, Jonathan. "The Gentle Way: Strikeforce Champion Ronda Rousey and the Birth of a Judo Star." Bleacher Report. April 6, 2012. http://bleacherreport.com/articles/1134250-the-gentle-way-strikeforce-champion-ronda-rousey-and-the-birth-of-a-judo-star

Svrluga, Barry and Liz Clarke. "Olympians struggle to adjust to life beyond the rings." *Washington Post*. August 20, 2016. https://www.washingtonpost.com/sports/olympics/olympians-struggle-to-adjust-to-life-beyond-the-rings/2016/08/20/9222dd98-66d1-11e6-be4e-23fc4d4d12b4_story.html?utm_term=.98377fb00571

Thamel, Pete. "Rousey's Journey Out of Pain, Through Judo." *New York Times*. August 11, 2008. http://www.nytimes.com/2008/08/12/sports/olympics/12judo.html

Wertheim, Jon. "The unbreakable Ronda Rousey is the world's most dominant athlete." *Sports Illustrated*. May 12, 2015. http://www.si.com/mma/2015/05/12/ronda-rousey-ufc-mma-fighter-armbar

Wetzel, Dan. "Dana White's about-face on women's MMA became official one historic night last August." Yahoo Sports. February 19, 2013. http://sports.yahoo.com/news/mma--dana-white-s-about-face-on-women-s-mma-became-official-one-historic-night-last-august-045153399.html

Zidan, Karim. "Serena Williams on Ronda Rousey: 'She was going for something totally different than I was.'" SB Nation. January 20, 2016. http://www.bloodyelbow.com/2016/1/20/10797796/serena-williams-ronda-rousey-something-totally-different-mma-tennis-australian-open

Further Information

Books

De Mars, AnnMaria, and James Pedro Sr. *Winning on the Ground: Training and Techniques for Judo and MMA Fighters.* Chicago, IL: Black Belt Communications, 2013.

Rousey, Ronda, and Maria Burns Ortiz, *My Fight/Your Fight.* New York: Regan Arts, 2015.

Straka, Mike. *Ronda Rousey's Fight to the Top.* Chicago, IL: Triumph Books, 2015

Online Articles

Grinberg, Emanuella. "Why UFC 'Beast' Ronda Rousey is such a big deal." CNN. August 5, 2015. http://edition.cnn.com/2015/08/02/living/ronda-rousey-profile-feat

Pilon, Mary. "Caged: What Drives Ronda Rousey to Wake Up and Fight." *Esquire.* November 10, 2015. http://www.esquire.com/sports/a39499/ronda-rousey-esquire-1115/

Sanneh, Kelefa. "Mean Girl." *New Yorker.* July 28, 2014. http://www.newyorker.com/magazine/2014/07/28/mean-girl

Shelburne, Ramona. "Rousey Says She's Down But Not Out." *ESPN The Magazine.* December 8, 2015. http://www.espn.com/espn/feature/story/_/page/espnwrousey/in-exclusive-interview-ronda-rousey-says-not-losing-holly-holm

Thamel, Pete. "Rousey's Journey Out of Pain, Through Judo." *New York Times*. August 11, 2008. http://www.nytimes. com/2008/08/12/sports/olympics/12judo.html

Videos

All Access: Ronda Rousey — Episode 1

https://www.youtube.com/watch?v=fJwdEMA-l_Y
A behind-the-scenes look at Ronda Rousey prior to her final Strikeforce fight, produced by Showtime.

Ronda Rousey Discusses Her UFC Upset

https://www.youtube.com/watch?v=iwCdv9iR8P8
Ronda Rousey talks about her loss to Holly Holm in 2015 with Ellen DeGeneres on *The Ellen Show*

Ronda Rousey's Sensitive Side

https://www.youtube.com/watch?v=29VNqy1AfjY
In her first appearance on *The Ellen Show*, Ronda Rousey discusses fight prep and her sensitive side.

Index

Page numbers in **boldface** are illustrations. Entries in **boldface** are glossary terms.

About the Author

Kevin Snow is a Canadian-born freelance writer now based in Buffalo, NY. He's covered everything from professional hockey to professional wrestling in his more than twenty years on the job. Snow was the Sports Editor of *TV Guide Canada* in the late 1990s, spent ten years with the NHL's Buffalo Sabres in their public relations and web departments, and has also written for both the Associated Press and Canadian Press.